F HORN BOOK 2

ESSENTIAL ELEMENTS for Band

COMPREHENSIVE BAND METHOD

TIM LAUTZENHEISER • JOHN HIGGINS • CHARLES MENGHINI
PAUL LAVENDER • TOM C. RHODES • DON BIERSCHENK

To create an account, visit:
www.essentialelementsinteractive.com

Student Activation Code
E2FH-5104-9998-7384

ISBN 979-835013683-8

REVIEW
KEY SIGNATURE
Key of F
TIME SIGNATURES
BREATH MARK
E F G A B♭ C D
NOTES
RESTS
Whole
Half
Quarter
Eighths
REPEAT SIGN
TIE
SLUR
TEMPO MARKINGS
Allegro
Moderato
1. TECHNIQUE TRAX
2. WELCOME SONG
African Folk Song
Allegro
mf
3. THAILAND LULLABY
See inside front cover for information on accessing instructional videos.
Thai Folk Song
Moderato
4. SHEPHERD'S HEY
English Folk Song
Moderato
5. THE CRAWDAD SONG
American Folk Song
Allegro

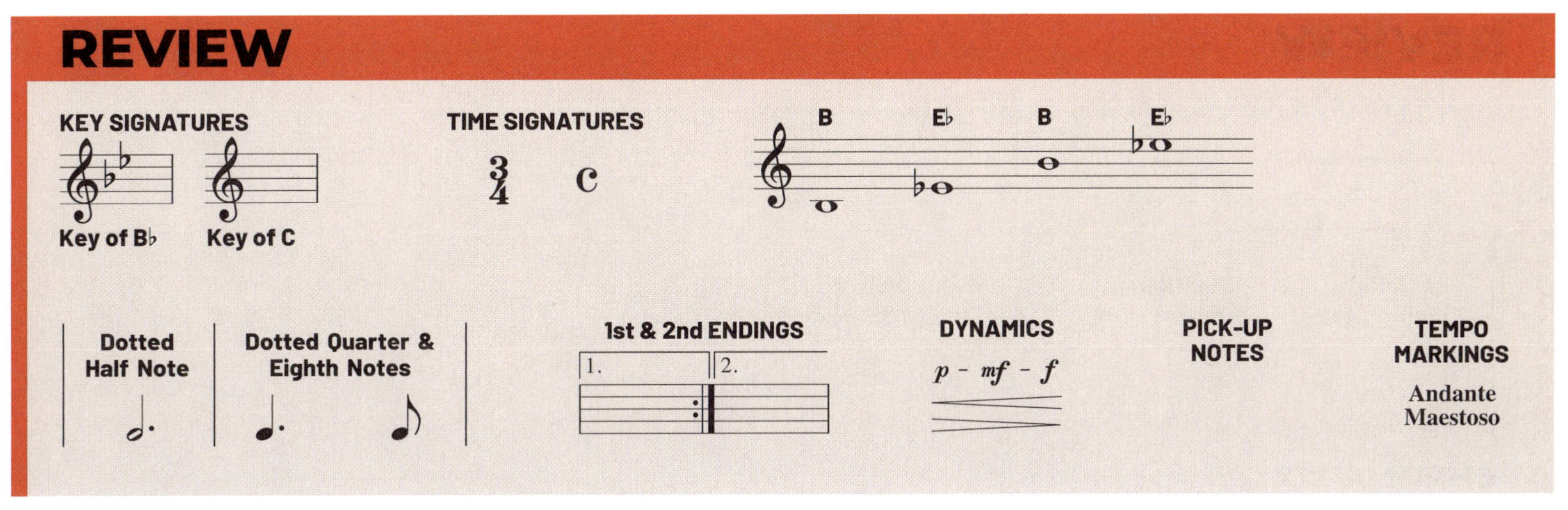

6. AMERICA/GOD SAVE THE QUEEN

Based on a Traditional Anthem

Andante

p

7. WEARING OF THE GREEN

Irish Folk Song

Moderato

mf

8. ROSES FROM THE SOUTH

Johann Strauss, Jr.

Allegro

f *p* *f*

1. 2.

p

9. CRUISIN' THROUGH THE PARK

Moderato

mf

1. 2.

10. TRUMPET VOLUNTARY – Duet

Jeremiah Clarke

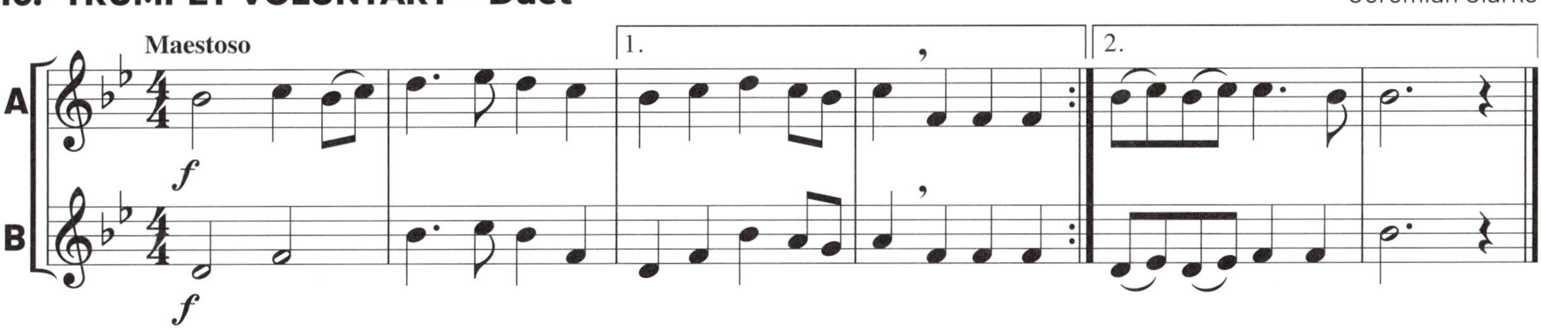

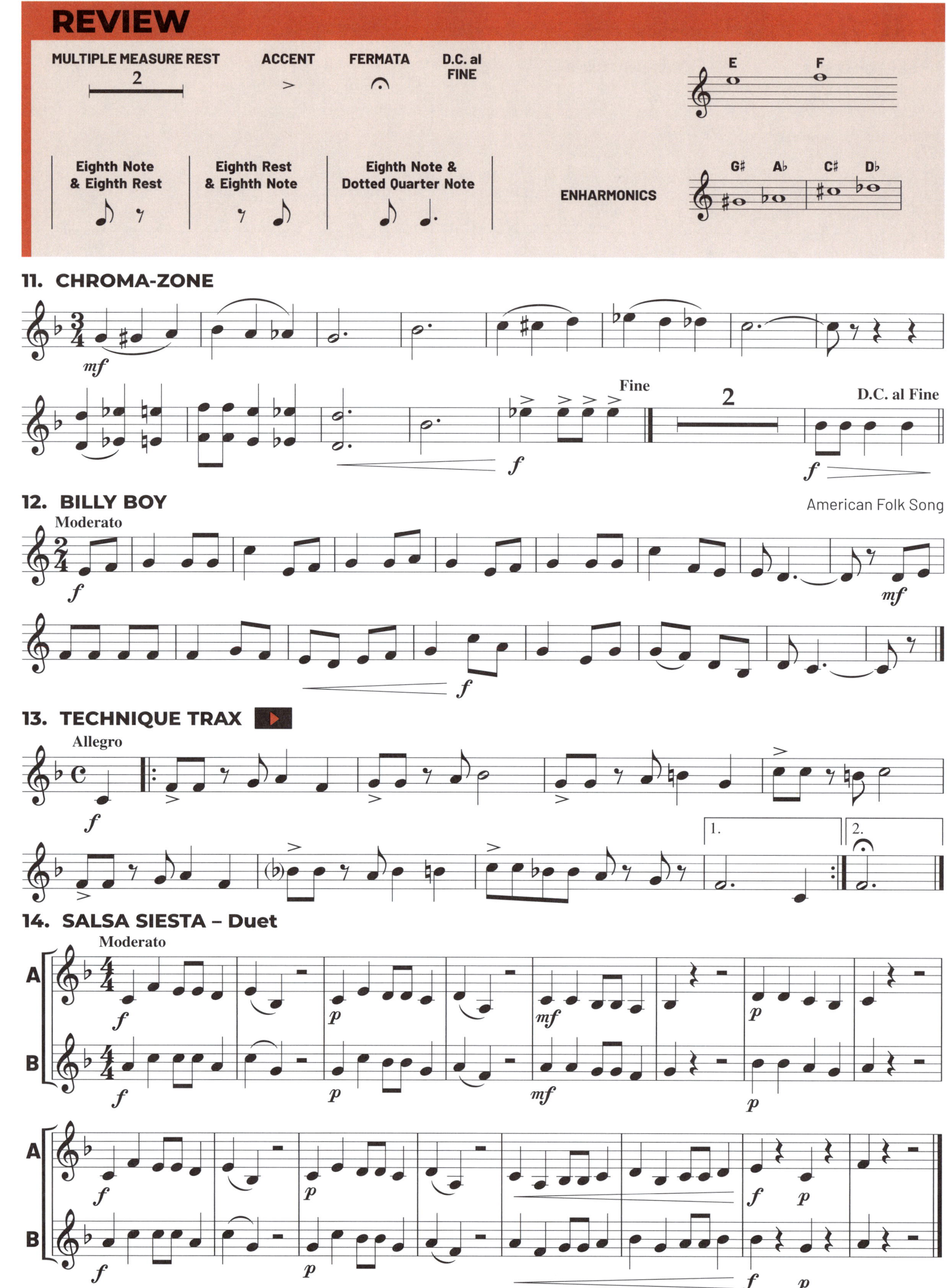
REVIEW
MULTIPLE MEASURE REST
2
ACCENT
FERMATA
D.C. al FINE
E
F
Eighth Note & Eighth Rest
Eighth Rest & Eighth Note
Eighth Note & Dotted Quarter Note
ENHARMONICS
G♯
A♭
C♯
D♭
11. CHROMA-ZONE
mf
Fine
2
D.C. al Fine
f
12. BILLY BOY
American Folk Song
Moderato
f
mf
13. TECHNIQUE TRAX
Allegro
f
1.
2.
14. SALSA SIESTA – Duet
Moderato
A
B
p
f

Staccato

Staccato notes are played lightly and with separation. They are marked with a dot above or below the note.

15. TREADING LIGHTLY

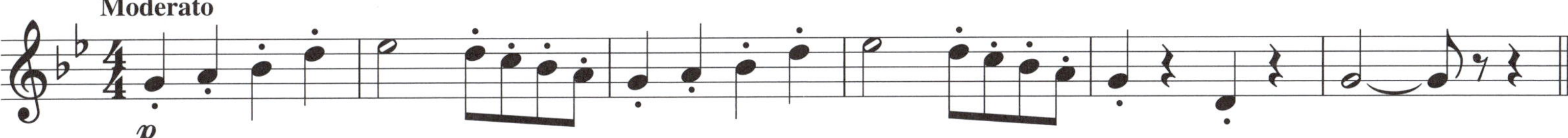

Tenuto

Tenuto notes are played smoothly and connected, holding each note until the next is played. They are marked with a straight line above or below the note.

16. SMOOTH MOVE

17. SHIFTING GEARS

HISTORY

English composer **Thomas Tallis** (1508–1585) served as a royal court composer for Kings Henry VIII and Edward VI, and Queens Mary and Elizabeth. During Tallis' lifetime, the artist Michelangelo painted the Sistine Chapel.

Canons (one or more parts imitating the first part) were used in many forms by 16th century composers. A **Round** is a strict (or exact) canon which can be repeated any number of times without stopping. Play *Tallis Canon* as a 4-part round.

18. TALLIS CANON (Round)

Thomas Tallis

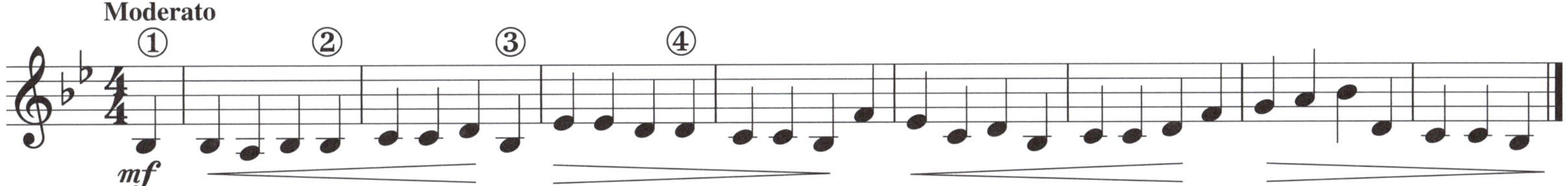

Sightreading

Sightreading means playing a musical piece for the first time. The key to sightreading success is to know what to look for *before* you play. Use the word **S-T-A-R-S** to remind yourself what to look for, and eventually your band will become sightreading STARS!

S – **Sharps or flats** in the key signature
T – **Time signature** and **tempo markings**
A – **Accidentals** not found in the key signature
R – **Rhythms**, silently counting the more difficult notes and rests
S – **Signs**, including dynamics, articulations, repeats and endings

19. SIGHTREADING CHALLENGE

DAILY WARM-UPS

WORK-OUTS FOR TONE & TECHNIQUE

20. TONE BUILDER

21. FLEXIBILITY STUDY

22. TECHNIQUE TRAX

23. CHORALE

Johann Sebastian Bach

Andante

p *mf* *p*

24. GRANDFATHER'S CLOCK

Henry C. Work

Ritardando *ritard.* (or) *rit.* – Gradually slower.

25. GLOW WORM

Paul Lincke

26. ALMA MATER

A.C. Weekes, W.M. Smith, H.S. Thompson

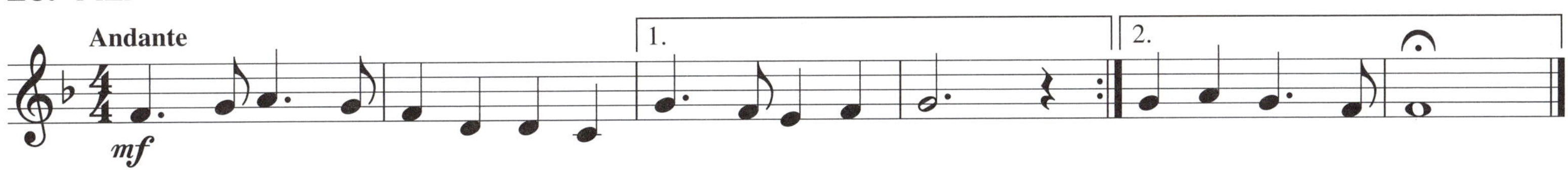

The Scottish folk song *Loch Lomond* is credited to an anonymous soldier who was imprisoned and awaiting execution. In it he writes of his desire to return home to his family and the breathtaking beauty of Loch (Lake) Lomond, a lake in Scotland. Located in the southern highlands, the lake is almost entirely surrounded by hills. One of these is Ben Lomond, a peak 3,192 feet high.

HISTORY

27. LOCH LOMOND

Scottish Folk Song

Key Changes

If a key signature changes during a piece of music, you will usually see a thin double bar line at the **key change**. You may also see natural signs reminding you to "cancel" previous sharps or flats. Keep playing, using the correct notes indicated in the *new* key signature.

THEORY

28. MOLLY MALONE

Irish Folk Song

Dynamics

cresc.	=	crescendo	(or)	(crescendo hairpin)
decresc.	=	decrescendo	(or)	(decrescendo hairpin)

29. RISE AND FALL

30. NO COMPARISON

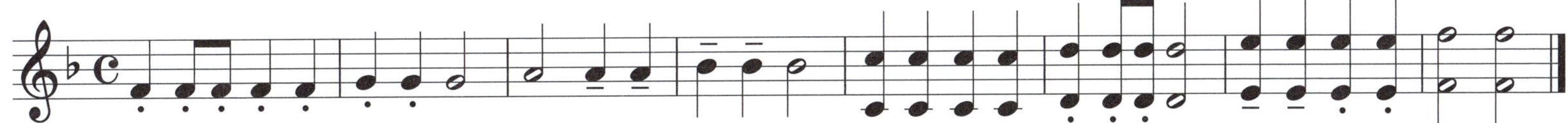

31. SIGHTREADING CHALLENGE

Remember the S-T-A-R-S guidelines.

THEORY
¢ Time Signature
Cut Time (Alla Breve)
or
= 2 beats per measure
= Half note gets one beat
= 2 beats
= 1 beat
= ½ beat
32. RHYTHM RAP Clap the rhythm while counting and tapping.
Clap
33. A CUT ABOVE
34. TWO-FOUR YANKEE DOODLE
American Folk Song
Moderato
mf
35. CUT TIME YANKEE DOODLE
American Folk Song
Moderato
mf
36. MARIANNE
Jamaican Folk Song
Moderato
p cresc.
f decresc.
p
37. THE VICTORS
Louis Elbel
March Tempo
f
Count ► 1 & 2 &
38. ESSENTIAL CREATIVITY Write this example in cut time ¢ before playing.
Allegro
f
Allegro

Dynamics

mp — *mezzo piano* (moderately soft)

Use full breath support at all dynamic levels.
p – *mp* – *mf* – *f*

39. A - ROVING

Syncopation

Syncopation occurs when an accent or emphasis is given to a note that is not on a strong beat. This type of "off-beat" feel is common in many popular and classical styles.

THEORY

40. RHYTHM RAP

41. IN SYNC

42. LA ROCA

Puerto Rican Folk Song

American composer **George M. Cohan** (1878–1942) was also a popular author, producer, director and performer. He helped develop a popular form of American musical theater now known as musical comedy. He is also considered to be one of the most famous composers of American patriotic songs, earning the Congressional Medal of Honor in 1917 for his song *Over There*. Many of his songs became morale boosters when the United States entered World War I in that same year.

HISTORY

43. ESSENTIAL ELEMENTS QUIZ – YOU'RE A GRAND OLD FLAG

Words and Music by George M. Cohan

This key signature indicates your **Key of G** (Concert C). Play all F's as F-sharp.

44. KEY MOMENT – New Note *Practice long tones on all new notes.*

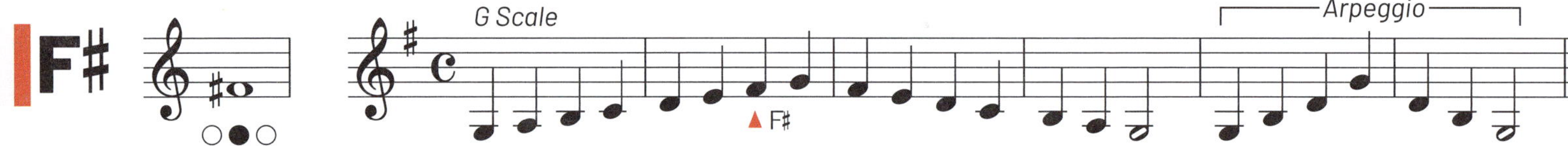

45. THE MINSTREL BOY

Irish Folk Song

46. CLOSE CALL – New Note

47. VICTORY MARCH

M. J. Shea

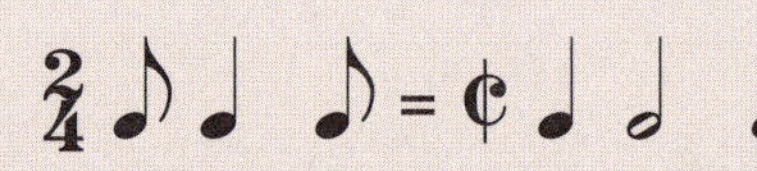

Compare the notation of the melody below with *Victory March* above. Should they sound the same?

48. WINNING STREAK

M. J. Shea

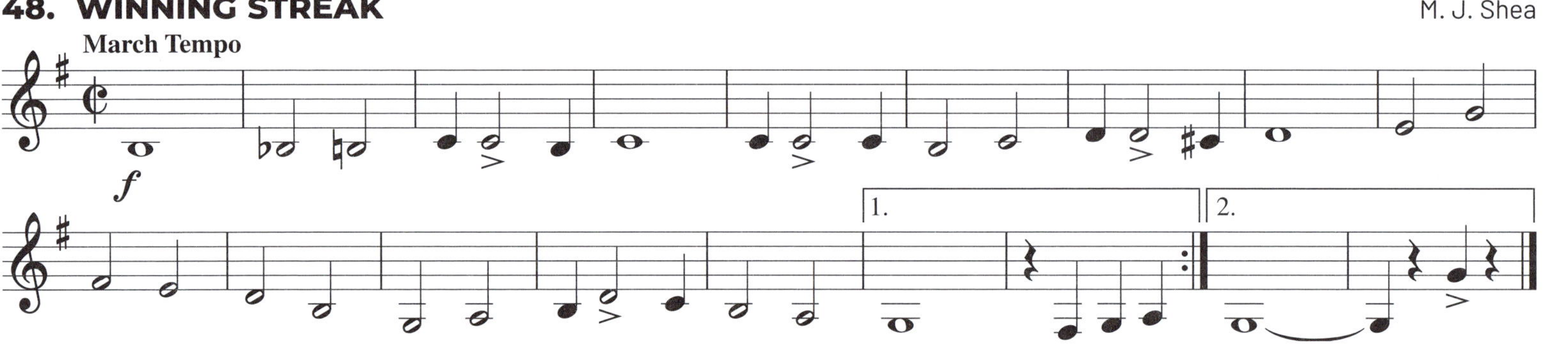

49. SIGHTREADING CHALLENGE *Remember the S-T-A-R-S guidelines.*

Sixteenth Notes

4 sixteenth notes = 1 Beat
Each sixteenth note = $\frac{1}{4}$ Beat

1 e & a

1 e & a 2 e & a

A single sixteenth note has 2 flags on the stem.

50. RHYTHM RAP

Clap

1 & 2 & 3 e & a 4 & | 1 & 2 & 3 e & a 4 & | 1 & 2 e & a 3 & 4 & | 1 & 2 e & a 3 & 4 &

51. SIXTEENTH NOTE FANFARE

1 & 2 & 3 e & a 4 & | 1 & 2 & 3 e & a 4 & | 1 & 2 e & a 3 & 4 & | 1 & 2 e & a 3 & 4 &

52. MOVING ALONG

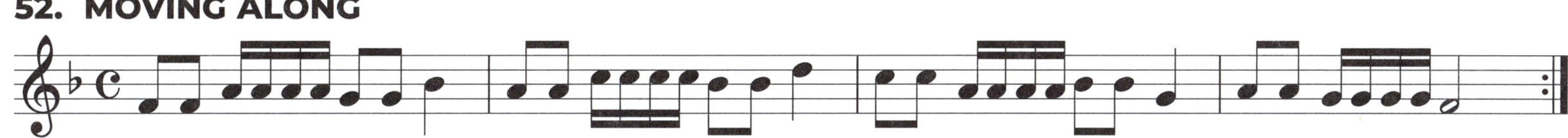

53. BACK AND FORTH – Duet

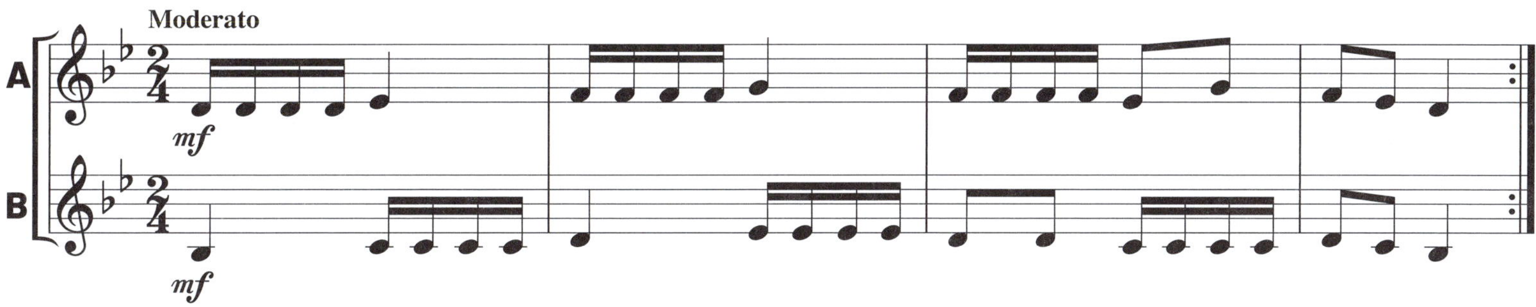

54. COMIN' ROUND THE MOUNTAIN VARIATIONS

American Folk Song

55. ESSENTIAL ELEMENTS QUIZ

PERFORMANCE SPOTLIGHT

PERFORMANCE SPOTLIGHT

63. RHYTHM RAP
Clap
1 & 2 & 3 e & a 4 & 1 & 2 & 3 & a 4 & 1 & 2 e & a 3 & a 4 & 1 & a 2 & a 3 & 4 &
64. SIXTEENTH VARIATIONS
1 & 2 & 3 e & a 4 & 1 & 2 & 3 & a 4 & 1 & 2 e & a 3 & a 4 & 1 & a 2 & a 3 & 4 &
65. SEA CHANTEY
Moderato
mp
cresc.
f
66. AMERICAN FANFARE
Maestoso
f
THEORY
New Key Signature
This key signature indicates your **Key of E♭** (Concert A♭).
Play all B's as B-flat, all E's as E-flat, and all A's as A-flat.
67. SCALE STUDY
E♭ Scale
68. BILL BAILEY
Hughie Cannon
Moderato
f
17

69. RHYTHM RAP

70. RHYTHM ETUDE

71. BATTLE STATIONS

72. ENGLISH DANCE

73. BIG ROCK CANDY MOUNTAIN

American Folk Song

74. ESSENTIAL ELEMENTS QUIZ

Moderato

f

Fine

D.C. al Fine

mp

Looking for some more fun music to play?
See the inside front cover for instructions on accessing recent popular Bonus Songs.

Rallentando *rall.* - Gradually slower (same as *ritardando*).

75. SIMPLE SONG – Duet

76. LINE DANCE

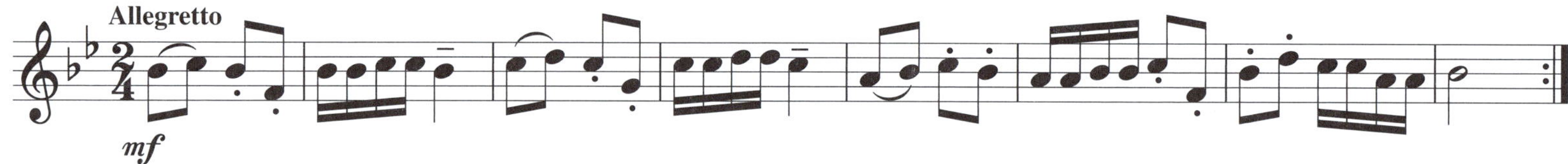

77. TECHNIQUE TRAX

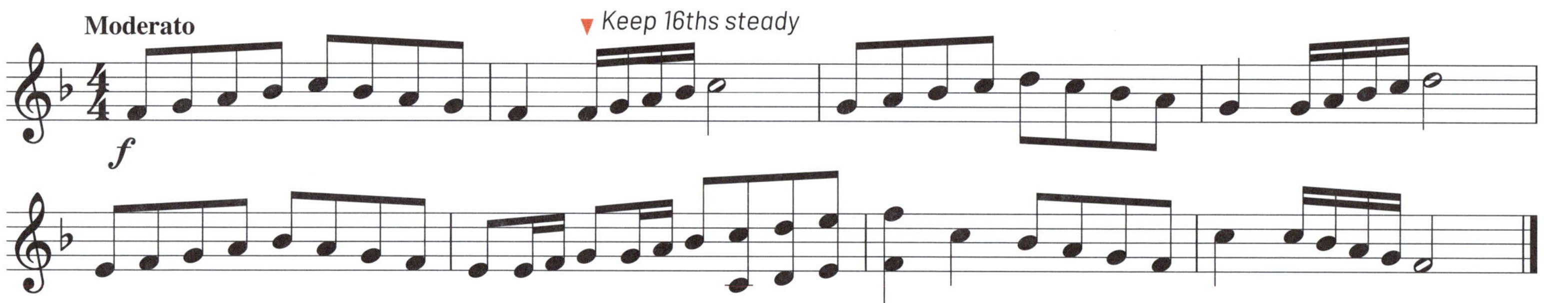

78. THE GALWAY PIPER

Irish Reel

79. MANHATTAN BEACH MARCH

John Philip Sousa

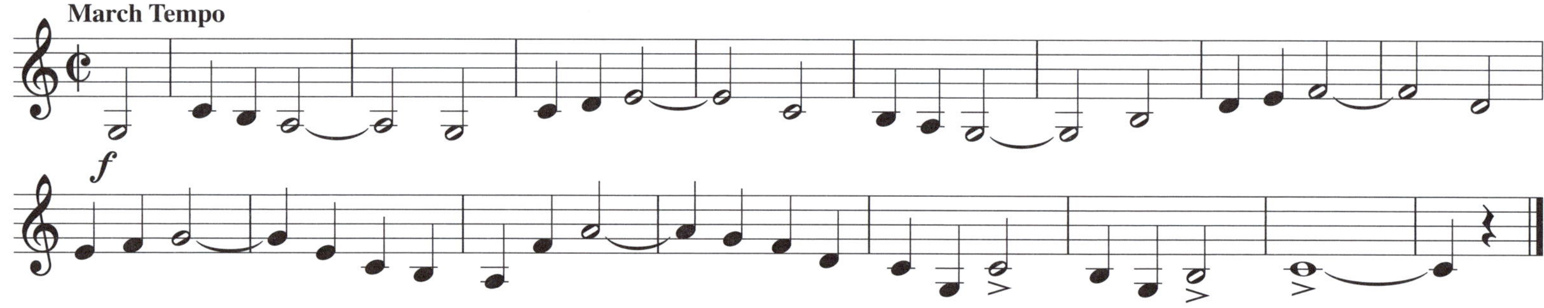

80. SIGHTREADING CHALLENGE *Remember the S-T-A-R-S guidelines.*

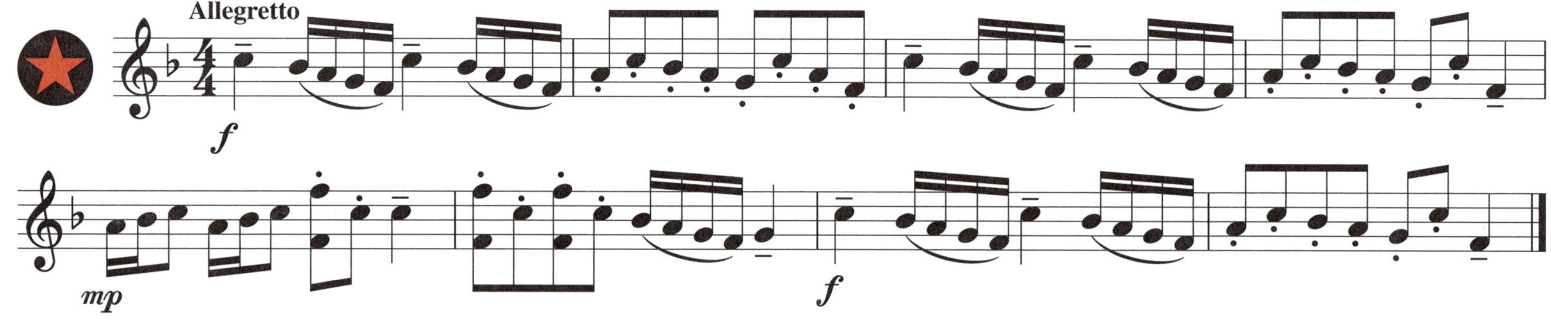

81. RHYTHM RAP
Clap
1 e & a 2 & 3 & a 4 & 1 & a 2 & 3 & a 4 & 1 & a 2 & 3 & a 4 & 1 & a 2 & 3 & 4 &
82. MARCHING ALONG
1 e & a 2 & 3 & a 4 & 1 & a 2 & 3 & a 4 & 1 & a 2 & 3 & a 4 & 1 & a 2 & 3 & 4 &
83. FANFARE FOR BAND – Trio
Maestoso
A
B
C
f
84. O TANNENBAUM
German Carol
Andante
mp
1.
2.
mf
f
rall.
85. S'VIVON
Traditional Hanukkah Song
Moderato
mf
f
mp
86. GOOD KING WENCESLAS
English Carol
Allegretto
mf
rit.

DAILY WARM-UPS

WORK-OUTS FOR TONE & TECHNIQUE

87. TONE BUILDER *Play at a very slow tempo.*

88. FLEXIBILITY STUDY

89. TECHNIQUE TRAX

90. CHORALE

Johann Sebastian Bach

Adagio

p mp p

mf mp rall. p

HISTORY

French composer **Georges Bizet** (1838–1875) entered the Paris Conservatory to study music when he was only ten years old. There he won many awards for voice, piano, organ, and composition. Bizet's best known composition is the opera *Carmen*, which was first performed in 1875. *Carmen* tells the story of a band of Gypsies, soldiers, smugglers, and outlaws. Originally criticized for its realism on stage, it was soon hailed as the most popular French opera ever written.

91. TOREADOR SONG (from CARMEN)

Georges Bizet

92. LA CUMPARSITA

G. Rodriguez

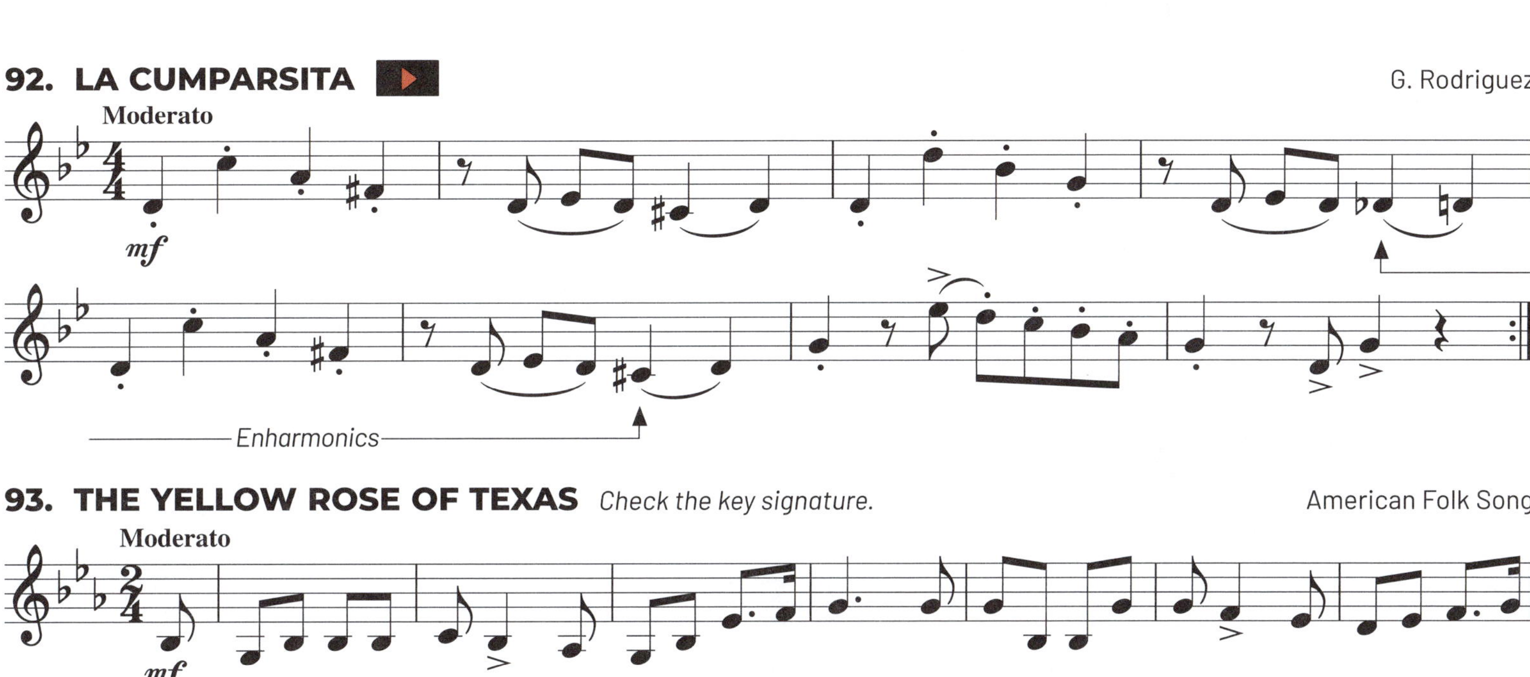

93. THE YELLOW ROSE OF TEXAS *Check the key signature.*

American Folk Song

94. SCALE STUDY

Until 1974 Australia's official national anthem was *God Save The Queen*. A competition was held in 1973 to compose a new anthem, but none of the entries met with the judges' approval. Finally the government asked the public to vote, choosing from among Australia's 3 most popular patriotic songs. After easily defeating *Waltzing Matilda* and *God Save The Queen*, *Advance Australia Fair* was officially declared the national anthem of Australia on April 19, 1974.

HISTORY

95. ADVANCE AUSTRALIA FAIR

Peter Dodds McCormick

Maestoso

f

9

mp cresc.

f

rit.

a tempo

Resume previous tempo

96. ESSENTIAL CREATIVITY

Arrange the melody of "America (My Country 'Tis Of Thee)" for your instrument. Write out the first line (6 measures). Your first note is C. ADD: Key signature—key of C • Time signature—3/4 • Tempo and dynamic markings.

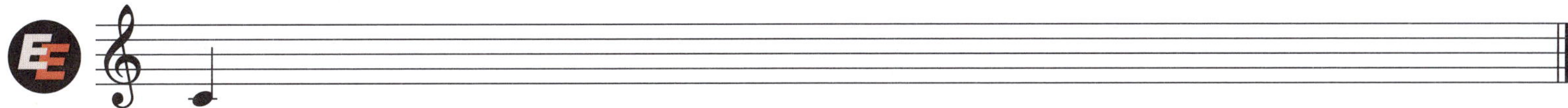

Play the completed line on your instrument to hear your own version.

97. AMERICAN PATROL
F. W. Meacham
Moderato
f
98. ARIA (from MARRIAGE OF FIGARO)
Wolfgang Amadeus Mozart
Moderato
mf
HISTORY
American composer John Philip Sousa (1854–1932) was best known for his brilliant band marches.
Sousa wrote 136 marches, including The Stars and Stripes Forever, which was declared the official march
of the United States of America in 1987.
99. THE STARS AND STRIPES FOREVER
John Philip Sousa
March Tempo
Check rhythm
f
17
Reproduced by Permission of Boosey & Hawkes Music Publishers Ltd.
100. SIGHTREADING CHALLENGE
Remember the S-T-A-R-S guidelines.
Moderato
mf
f

6/8 Time Signature

6/8 = **6 beats** per measure
= **Eighth** note gets one beat

♪ = 1 beat ♩ = 2 beats
♩. = 3 beats 𝅗𝅥. = 6 beats

THEORY

6/8 time is usually played with a slight emphasis on the **1st** and **4th** beats of each measure. This divides the measure into 2 groups of 3 beats each. In faster music, these two primary beats will make the music feel like it's counted "in 2."

101. RHYTHM RAP *Clap the rhythm while counting and tapping.*

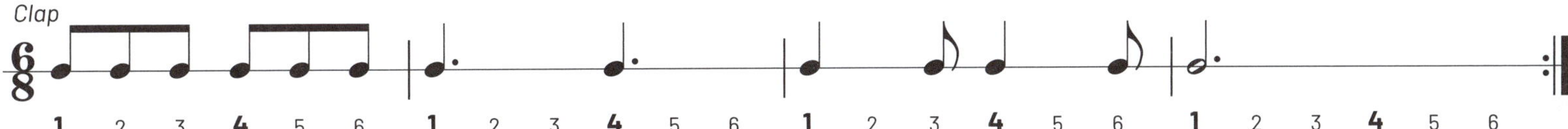

102. LAZY DAY

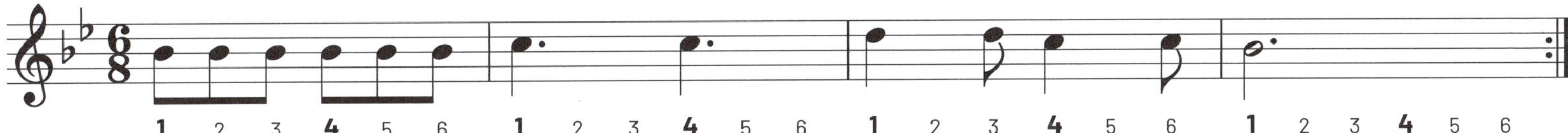

103. ROW YOUR BOAT

104. JOLLY GOOD FELLOW

105. CHANSON

French Folk Song

106. ESSENTIAL ELEMENTS QUIZ – WHEN JOHNNY COMES MARCHING HOME

American Folk Song

THEORY

More Enharmonics

Remember that notes which sound the same but have different letter names are called **enharmonics**. These are some common enharmonics that you'll use in the exercises below.

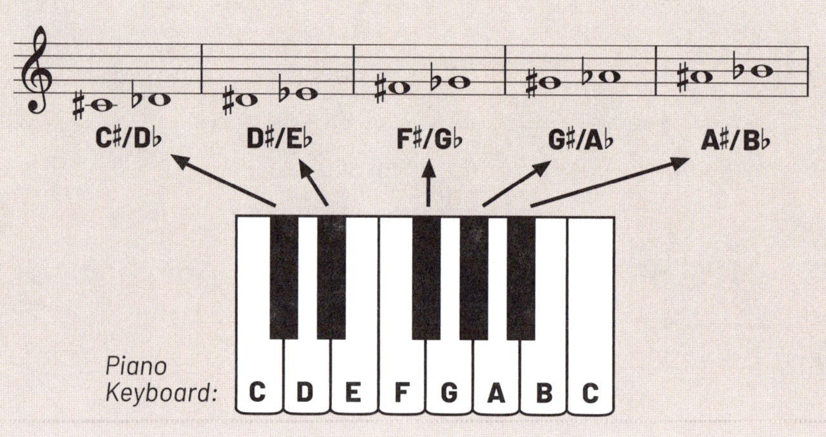

More Chromatics

The smallest distance between two notes is a half-step, and a scale made up of consecutive half-steps is a **chromatic scale**. These are usually written with **enharmonic** notes—sharps when going up and flats when going down.

107. CHROMATIC SCALE *Practice slowly until you are sure of all the fingerings.*

108. TECHNIQUE TRAX

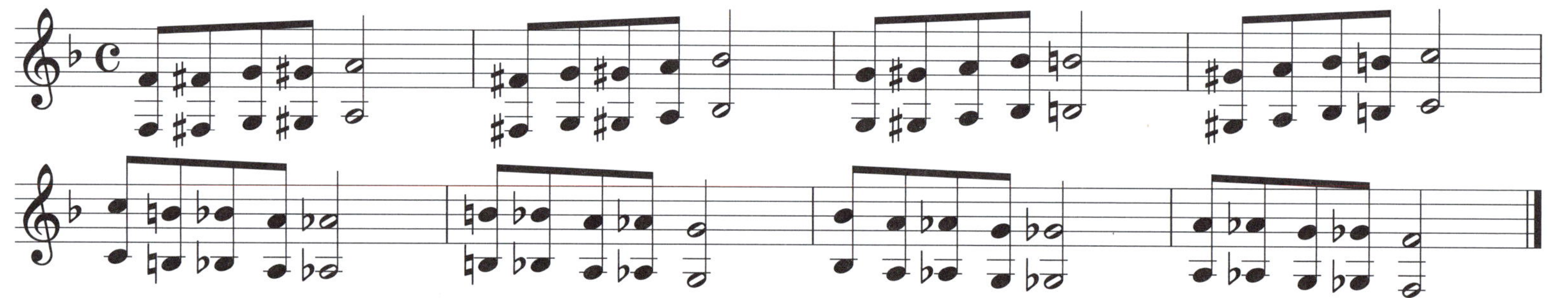

HISTORY

A **Habañera** is a Cuban dance and song form in slow 2/4 meter. It is named after the city of Havana, the capital of Cuba. Made popular in the New World in the early 19th Century, it was later carried over to Spain. There the rhythms of the Habañera were incorporated into many styles of Latin music. One of the most famous Habañeras is heard in Bizet's *Carmen*, written in 1875.

109. HABAÑERA (from CARMEN)

Georges Bizet

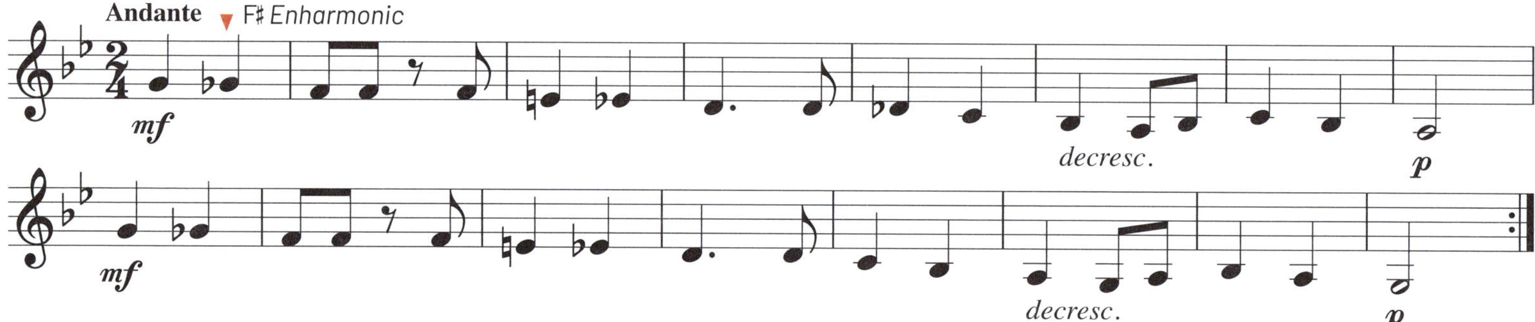

110. CHROMATIC CRESCENDO

111. TURKISH MARCH (from THE RUINS OF ATHENS)
Ludwig van Beethoven
Allegretto
mf
112. THE OVERLANDER
Australian Folk Song
Allegro
mp
113. STACCATO STUDY
Moderato
A♭ Enharmonic
F♯ Enharmonic
p
cresc.
f
decresc.
p
114. YANKEE DOODLE DANDY
Words and Music by George M. Cohan
Allegro
mf
mp
f
17
mf
mp
f
© 1904 E.B. Marks Music Corp., USA
B. Feldman & Co. Ltd., London WC2H 0QY (Brit. Comm. Excluding Australia and Canada, Eire, Europe, SA)
Reproduced by permission of IMP Ltd. All Rights Reserved
115. SIGHTREADING CHALLENGE
Remember the S-T-A-R-S guidelines:
S - Sharps or flats in the key signature, T - Time signature and tempos, A - Accidentals, R - Rhythm, S - Signs
Moderato
1.
2.
mf
f

THEORY

Triplets

A **triplet** is a group of **3** notes played in the space of **2**. In 2/4, 3/4, or 4/4 time, an eighth note triplet is spread evenly across one beat.

3 = 1 beat

1 trip-let **2** trip-let

116. RHYTHM RAP

Clap

1 2 3 trip-let 4 | 1 2 trip-let 3 4 | 1 trip-let 2 3 trip-let 4 | 1 trip-let 2 trip-let 3 4

117. THREE TO GET READY

118. TRIPLET STUDY

▲ A♭ *Enharmonic*

▲ *Check Rhythm*

119. MARCH (from THE NUTCRACKER) – Duet

Peter I. Tchaikovsky

Allegretto

A

B

mf

mp

f

120. ESSENTIAL ELEMENTS QUIZ – THEME FROM FAUST

Charles Gounod

121. SCALE STUDY

122. OVER THE RIVER AND THROUGH THE WOODS

American Folk Song

123. RHYTHM RAP

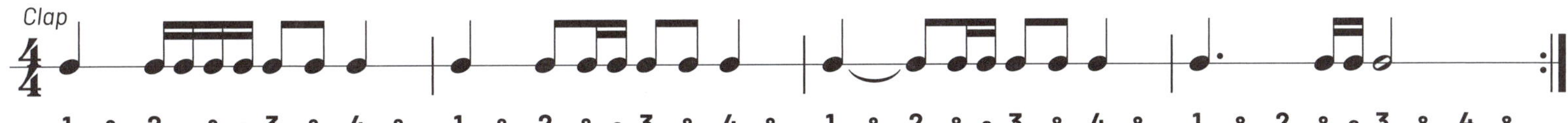

124. ON THE MOVE

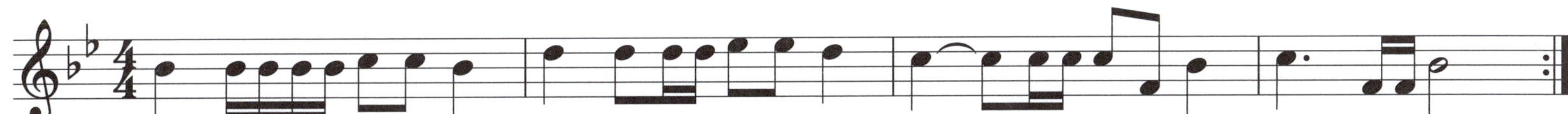

125. HIGHER GROUND

126. ESSENTIAL ELEMENTS QUIZ

HISTORY

The first known printing of the lyrics and music to **The Marines' Hymn** dates from August 1, 1918. An unknown author is believed to have taken the opening words of the song from the words on the Marine Corps flag, "From the halls of Montezuma to the shores of Tripoli." The music was taken from "Genevieve de Brabant," by the operetta composer Jacques Offenbach.

127. THE MARINES' HYMN

D.S. al Fine

Play until you see the **D.S. al Fine**. Then go back to the sign (𝄋) and play until the word **Fine**. **D.S.** is the abbreviation for **Dal Segno**, or "from the sign," and **Fine** means "the end."

128. D.S. MARCH

Accelerando

accel. – Gradually faster.

129. CAN-CAN

Jacques Offenbach

▲ *Watch your director.*

130. TARANTELLA

Italian Folk Song

The **waltz** is a dance in moderate 3/4 time which developed around 1800 from the Ländler, an Austrian peasant dance. Austrian composer **Johann Strauss, Jr.** (1825–1899) composed over 400 waltzes. These include such famous pieces as *The Blue Danube*, *Tales From the Vienna Woods* and *Emperor Waltz*.

HISTORY

131. EMPEROR WALTZ

Johann Strauss, Jr.

Legato Style

legato – Played in a smooth, connected style.

132. ENGLISH DANCE – Duet

Johann Christian Bach

133. ESSENTIAL ELEMENTS QUIZ – BRITISH GRENADIERS

Traditional

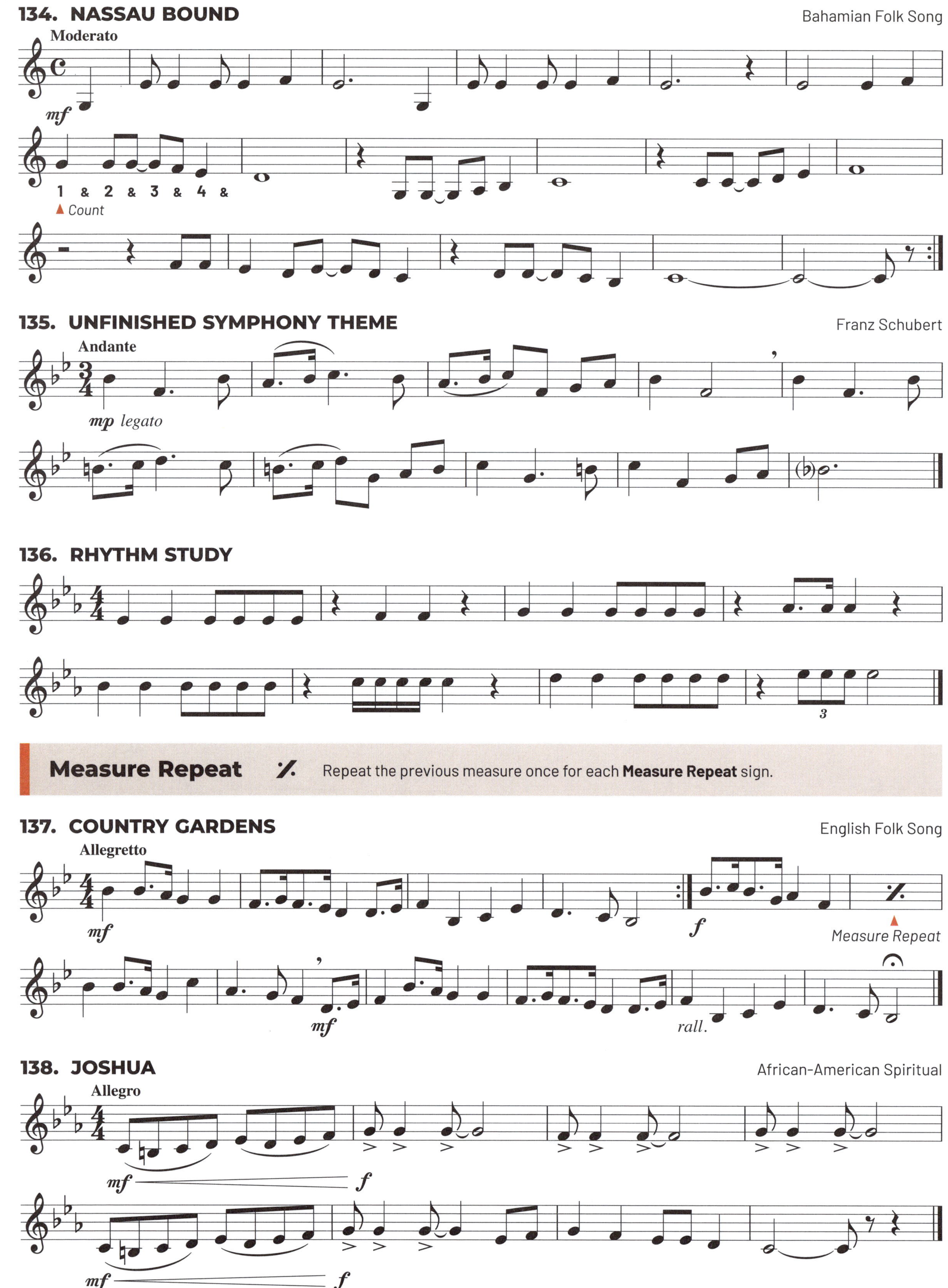
134. NASSAU BOUND
Bahamian Folk Song
Moderato
mf
1 & 2 & 3 & 4 &
Count
135. UNFINISHED SYMPHONY THEME
Franz Schubert
Andante
mp legato
136. RHYTHM STUDY
3
Measure Repeat
Repeat the previous measure once for each Measure Repeat sign.
137. COUNTRY GARDENS
English Folk Song
Allegretto
mf
f
Measure Repeat
mf
rall.
138. JOSHUA
African-American Spiritual
Allegro
mf
f
mf
f

139. LISTEN TO THE MOCKINGBIRD

Alice Hawthorne

Moderato

mf ▸ Pick-up

140. ANCHORS AWEIGH

Capt. A.H. Miles and C.A. Zimmerman

March Tempo

f *mf* *cresc.*

1. *f* 2. *f*

141. GREENSLEEVES

English Folk Song

Andante

p *mf*

rit.

142. THE LONG CLIMB

143. THE BLUE BELLS OF SCOTLAND

Scottish Folk Song

THEORY

Major and Minor

The scales you've already learned are called **Major** scales. They all follow the same pattern, with **half-steps** between notes 3-4 and between notes 7-8.

Natural Minor scales follow a different pattern, with **half-steps** between notes 2-3 and 5-6. The **D Minor** scale uses the same key signature as **F Major**.

Another type of minor scale is called **Harmonic Minor**, which adds an accidental to raise the **7th** note by a half-step. Compare the scales on the right.

See page 37 for additional minor scales.

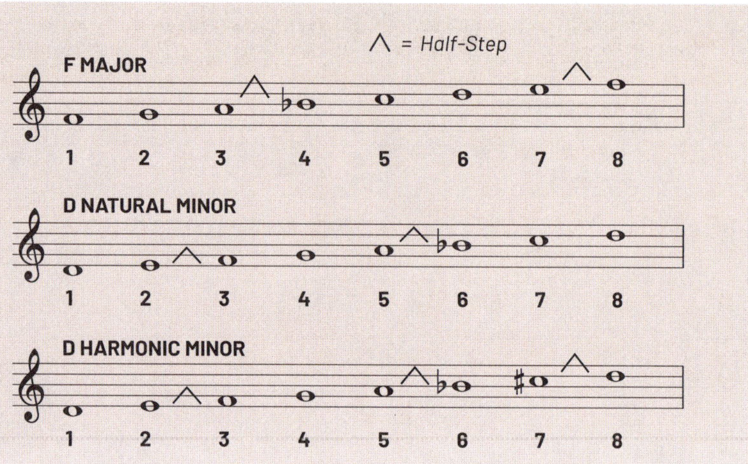

144. NATURAL MINOR SCALE

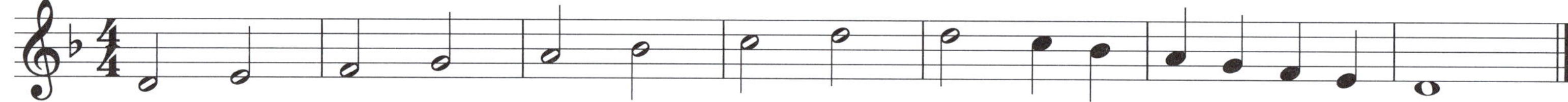

145. FINALE FROM "NEW WORLD SYMPHONY"

Antonin Dvorák

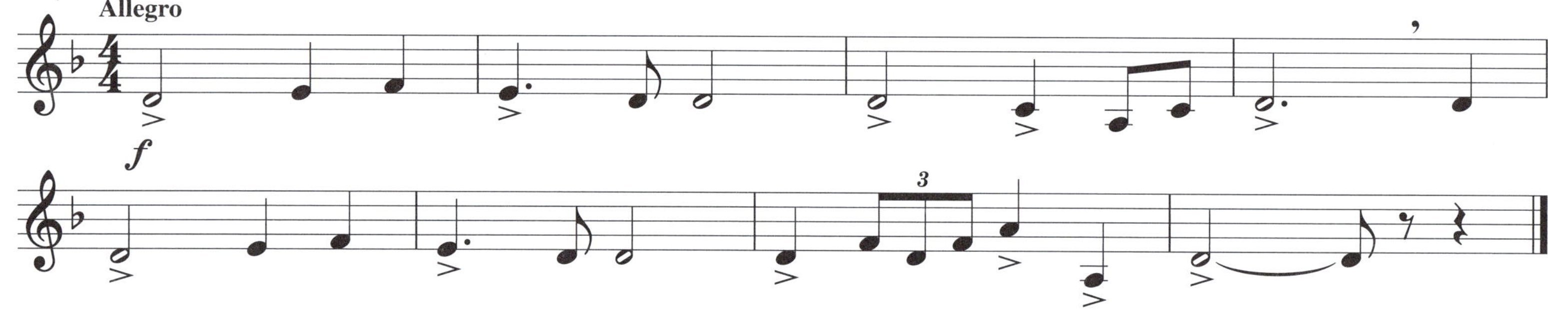

146. HARMONIC MINOR SCALE

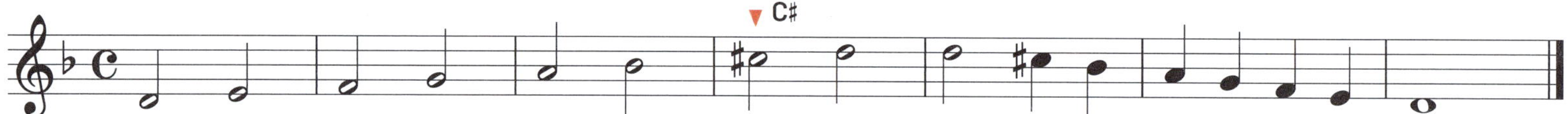

147. HUNGARIAN DANCE NO. 5

Johannes Brahms

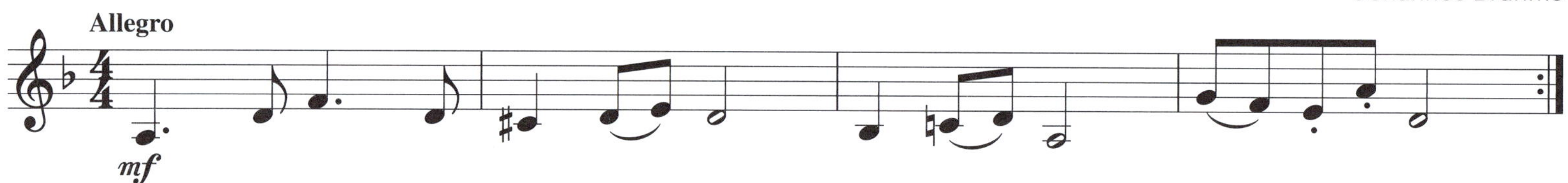

148. POMP AND CIRCUMSTANCE (LAND OF HOPE AND GLORY)

Edward Elgar

PERFORMANCE SPOTLIGHT

D.S. al Coda Play until you see the **D.S. al Coda**. Then go back to the sign (𝄋) and play until the **Coda Sign** ("To Coda" 𝄌). Skip directly to the **Coda** and play until the end.

149. SIMPLE GIFTS – Band Arrangement

Shaker Folk Song
Arr. by John Higgins

PERFORMANCE SPOTLIGHT

151. DANNY BOY – Band Arrangement

Irish Folk Song
Arr. by John Higgins

152. TAKE ME OUT TO THE BALL GAME – Band Arrangement

By Jack Norworth and Harry von Tilzer
Arr. by John Higgins

Additional Bonus Songs are available online. See the inside front cover for details.

PERFORMANCE SPOTLIGHT

153. SERENGETI (AFRICAN RHAPSODY) – Band Arrangement

John Higgins

Maestoso "Daybreak"

f *mp* *rit.*

5 Forceful *f*

3

9 "Safari" 10

19 *mf*

27 10

37 *f* *decresc.*

mp *rit.*

45 Moderately Fast 4

49 "Celebration"
Play 3 times
Play 2nd & 3rd time only

mf – f

Play all times

57 *mf*

mp *rit.*

65 "Sunset"
Slowly 3

p

RUBANK® STUDIES

154. CHORALE (Concert B♭)

155. CHORALE (Concert E♭)

156. CHORALE (Concert F)

157. CHORALE (Concert A♭)

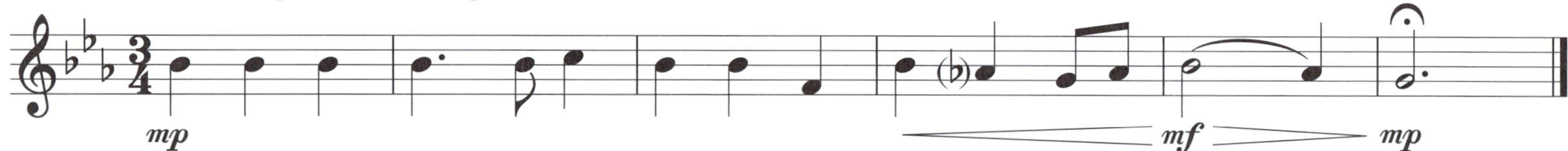

158. CHORALE (Concert C)

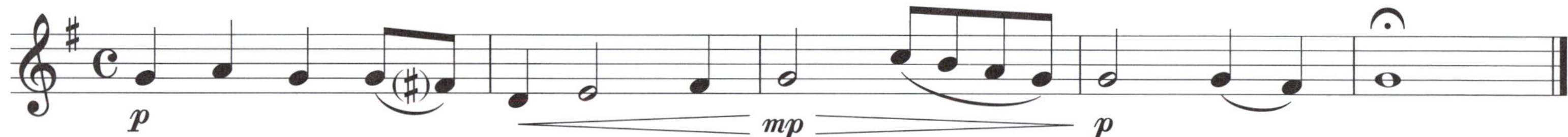

F HORN KEY OF F (Concert B♭)

159.

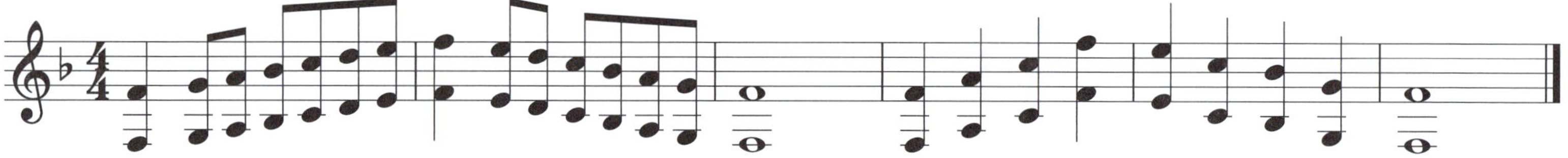

160.

161.

162.

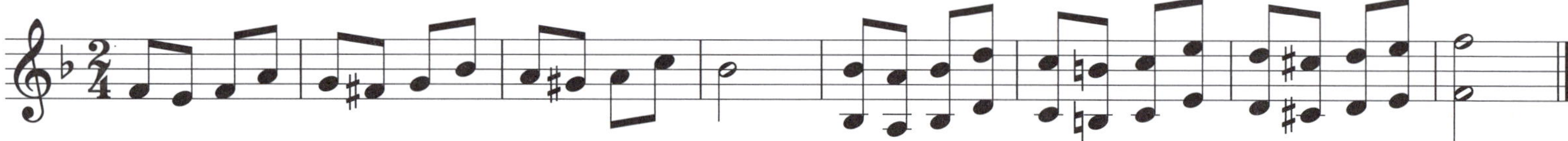

RUBANK® STUDIES

RUBANK® STUDIES

F HORN KEY OF E♭ (Concert A♭)

171.

172.

173.

174.

F HORN KEY OF G (Concert C)

175.

176.

177.

178.

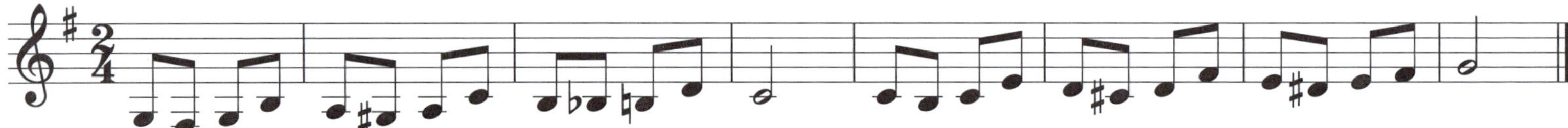

RUBANK® STUDIES

F HORN KEY OF D MINOR (CONCERT G MINOR)

F HORN KEY OF G MINOR (CONCERT C MINOR)

F HORN KEY OF A MINOR (CONCERT D MINOR)

CHROMATIC SCALES

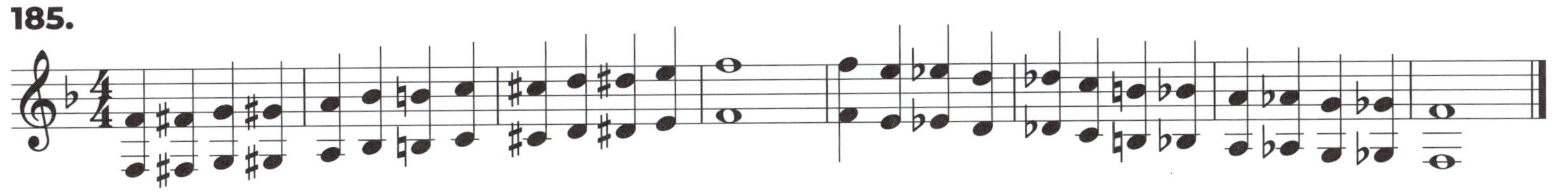

186.

INDIVIDUAL STUDY – F Horn

187. TONE BUILDER

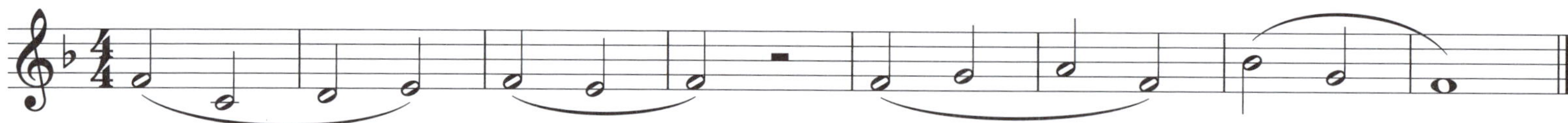

188. FLEXIBILITY STUDY

189. ARPEGGIO CHALLENGE

190. MELODY PATTERNS

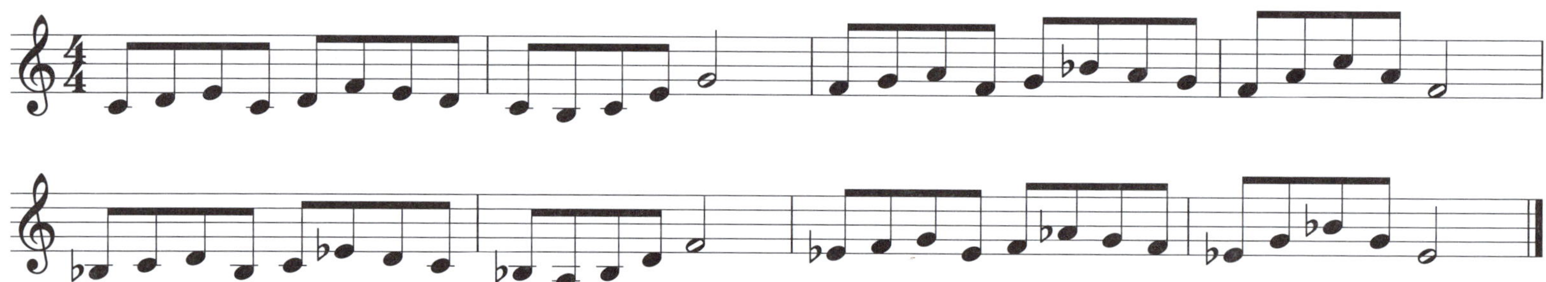

191. ARTICULATION WORK-OUT

INDIVIDUAL STUDY – F Horn

INDIVIDUAL STUDY – F Horn

Solo with Piano Accompaniment

You can perform this solo with the piano accompaniment on the following page.

197. ROMANZE from "Concerto No. 3, KV 447" – F Horn Solo

Online audio – see inside front cover to access.

Wolfgang Amadeus Mozart
Arr. by H. Voxman

INDIVIDUAL STUDY – F Horn

197. ROMANZE from "Concerto No. 3, KV 447" – Piano Accompaniment Wolfgang Amadeus Mozart
Online audio - see inside front cover to access. Arr. by H. Voxman

RHYTHM STUDIES

RHYTHM STUDIES

CREATING MUSIC

THEORY

Theme and Variation

Theme and Variation is a technique used by composers and arrangers to create interesting musical ideas that are "varied" from an established melody, or "theme." Play the following theme and two variations to hear how the arranger has created new phrases based on the original melody.

1. THEME

"Simple Gifts"

VARIATION 1 *Adding some notes • Changing some rhythms*

VARIATION 2 *Removing notes • Changing rhythms • Adding accents • Adding notes*

2. THEME AND YOUR VARIATION

Write your own variation of this theme. Use your instrument to hear and try different ideas.

"Candy Mountain Rock"

Theme

Your Variation

THEORY

Blues Improvisation

Improvisation using a **Blues Scale** is an important part of jazz and popular music. Musicians use combinations of these notes and various rhythms to create their own spontaneous solos over a 12 measure progression of chords.

Blues Scale

3. LET'S JAM

Use the indicated notes from the Blues Scale to create your own solo to play with the accompaniment (Line B).

You can mark your progress through the book on this page.
Fill in the stars as instructed by your band director.

1. Page 2–4, Review
2. Page 5, Sightreading Challenge, No. 19
3. Page 6, Daily Warm-Ups
4. Page 7, Sightreading Challenge, No. 31
5. Page 8, Essential Creativity, No. 38
6. Page 9, EE Quiz, No. 43
7. Page 10, Sightreading Challenge, No. 49
8. Page 11, EE Quiz, No. 55
9. Page 12–13, Performance Spotlight
10. Page 15, EE Quiz, No. 74
11. Page 16, Sightreading Challenge, No. 80
12. Page 18, Daily Warm-Ups
13. Page 19, Essential Creativity, No. 96
14. Page 20, Sightreading Challenge, No. 100
15. Page 21, EE Quiz, No. 106
16. Page 22, Chromatic Scale, No. 107
17. Page 23, Sightreading Challenge, No. 115
18. Page 24, EE Quiz, No. 120
19. Page 25, EE Quiz, No. 126
20. Page 27, EE Quiz, No. 133
21. Page 30, Natural Minor Scale, No. 144
22. Page 30, Harmonic Minor Scale, No. 146
23. Page 30, Pomp and Circumstance, No. 148
24. Page 31, Performance Spotlight
25. Page 32, Performance Spotlight
26. Page 33, Performance Spotlight
27. Page 38–39, Individual Study
28. Page 40, Performance Spotlight

MUSIC — AN ESSENTIAL ELEMENT OF LIFE

FINGERING CHART

F HORN

Instrument Care Reminders

Before putting your instrument back in its case after playing, do the following:

- Use the water key to empty water from the instrument. Blow air through it. If your horn does not have a water key, invert the instrument.
  You may also remove the main tuning slide, invert the instrument and remove excess water.
- Wipe the instrument off with a clean soft cloth. Return the instrument to its case.
- Remove the mouthpiece.
  Once a week, wash the mouthpiece with warm tap water. Dry thoroughly.

Be sure to grease the slides regularly. Your director will recommend special slide grease and valve oil, and will help you apply them when necessary.

CAUTION: If a slide, a valve or your mouthpiece becomes stuck, ask for help from your band director or music dealer. Special tools should be used to prevent damage to your instrument.

Using the Correct Fingering

Single Horn Players

- F Horn players use the upper fingerings - marked "F Horn"
- B♭ Horn players use the lower fingerings - marked "B♭ Horn"
  *The trigger key (**T**) is only used on double horns.

Double Horn Players

- The trigger key (**T**) allows double horn players to switch between F and B♭ Horn
- Use the "F Horn" fingering when the trigger key is **not** pressed.
  *For notes without a "**T**" fingering, the F Horn fingering is the recommended double horn fingering for that note.
- Use the "B♭ Horn" fingering when the trigger key is pressed.
  *For notes with a "**T**" fingering, the B♭ Horn fingering is the recommended double horn fingering for that note.

○ = Open
● = Pressed down
T = Trigger (Double Horn Only)

Instruments and photos courtesy of Yamaha.

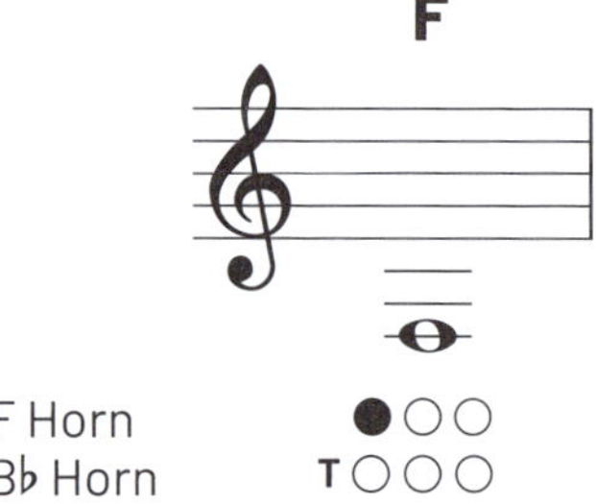

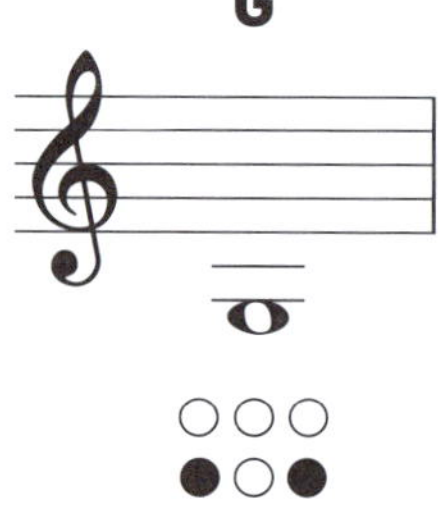

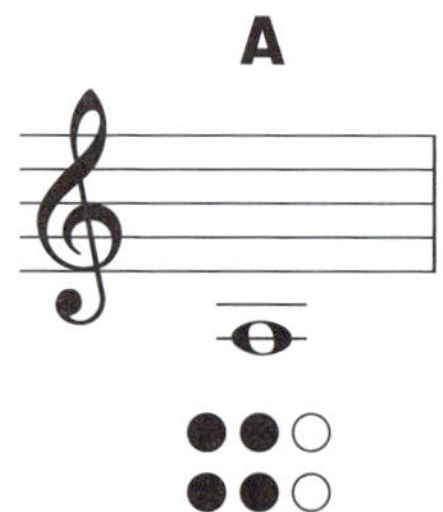

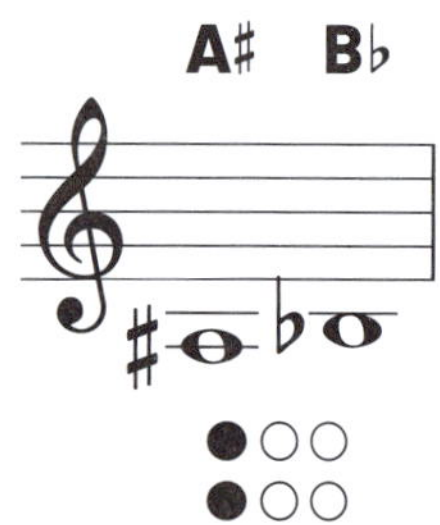

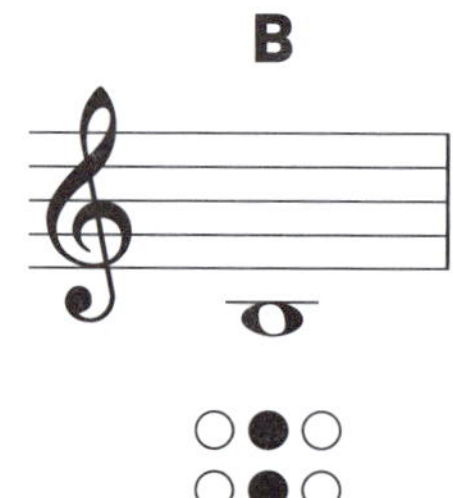

FINGERING CHART

F HORN

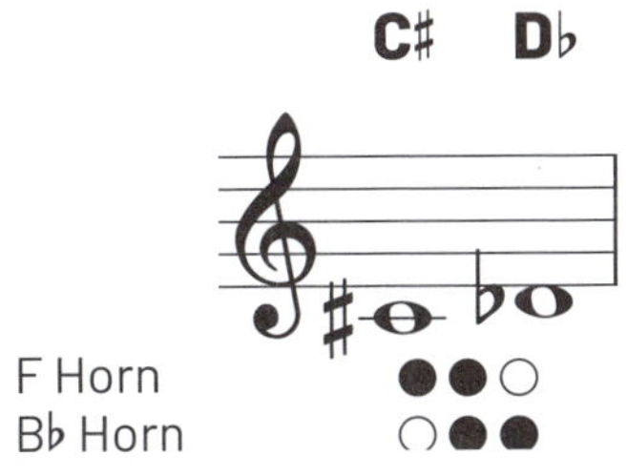

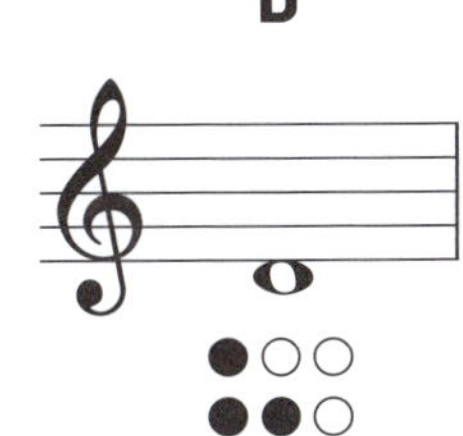

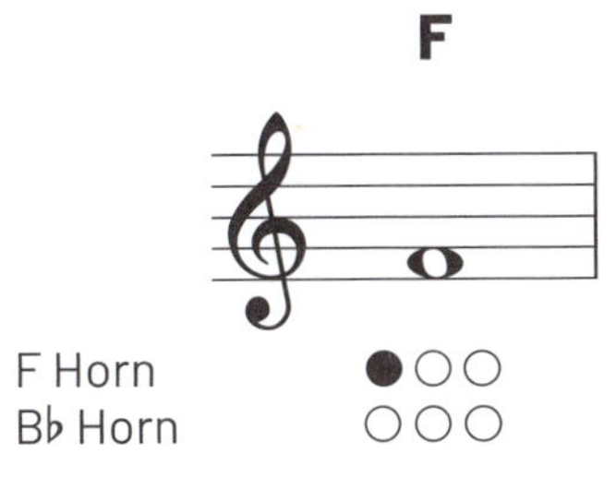

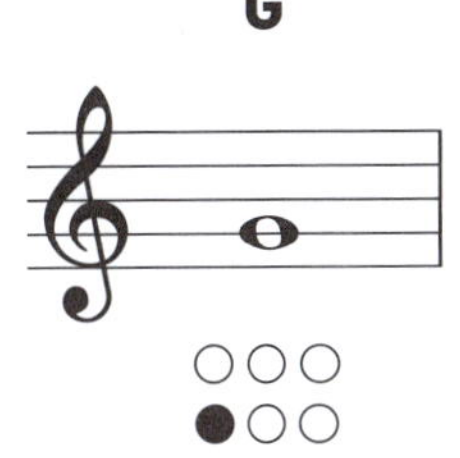

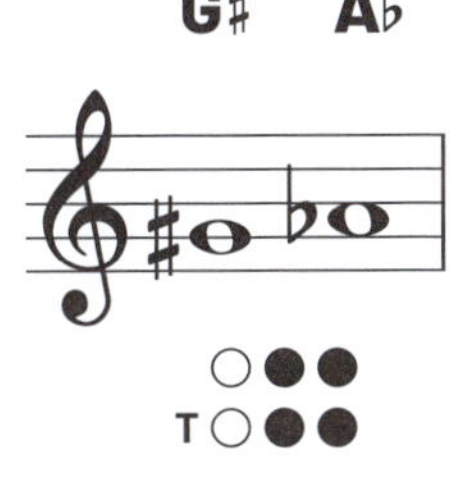

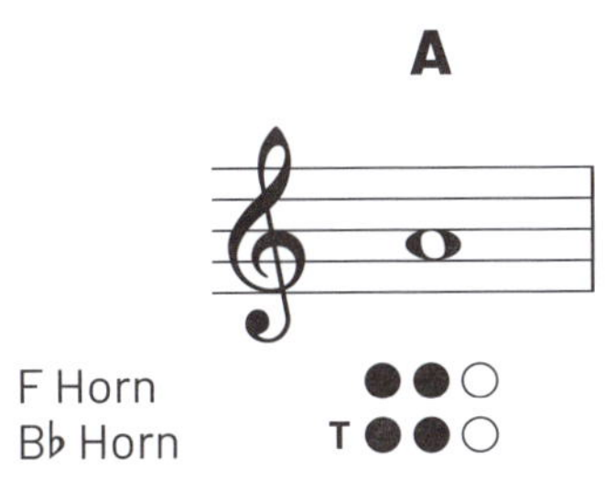

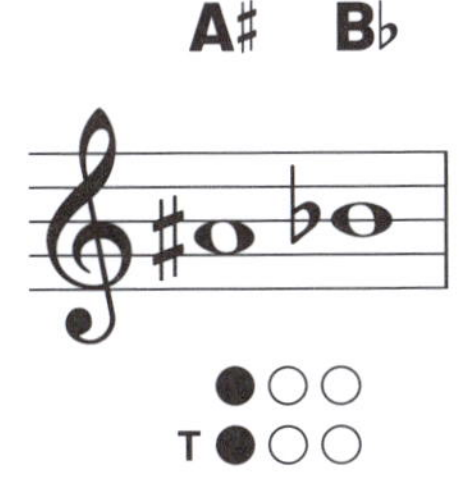

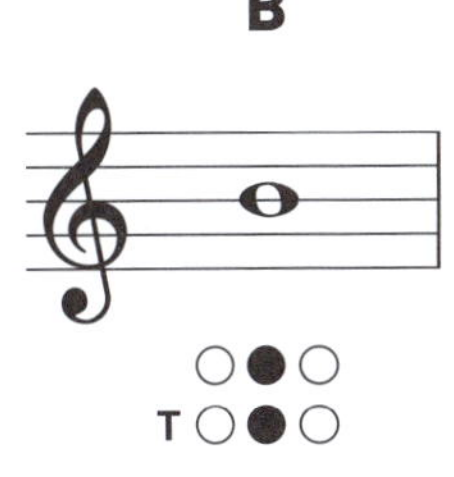

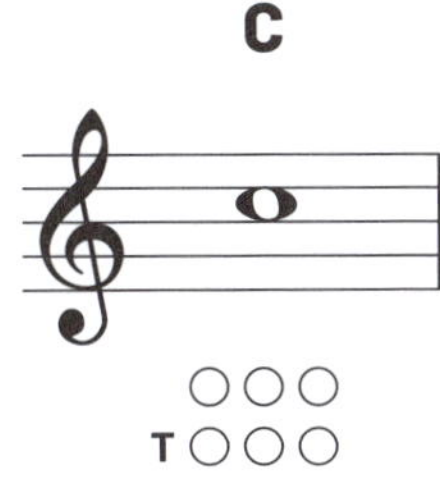

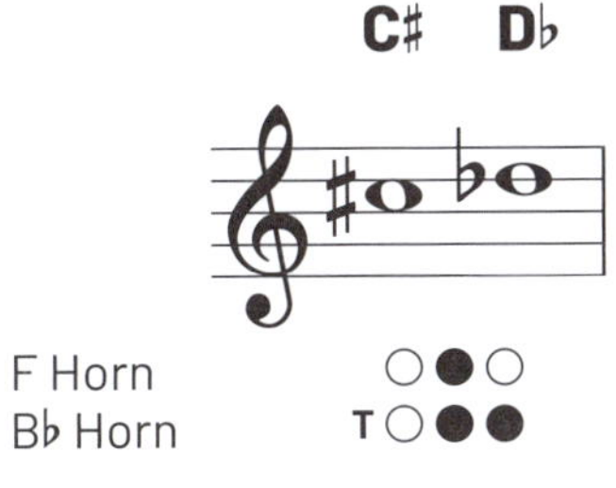

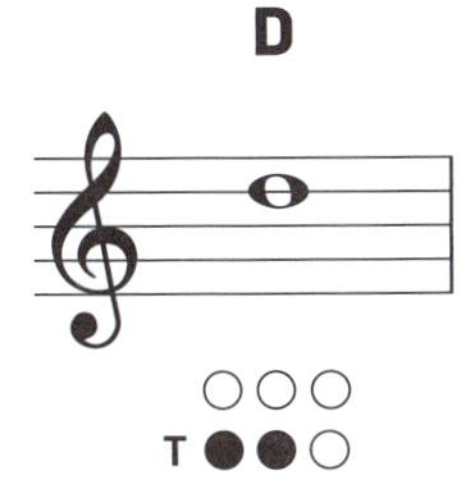

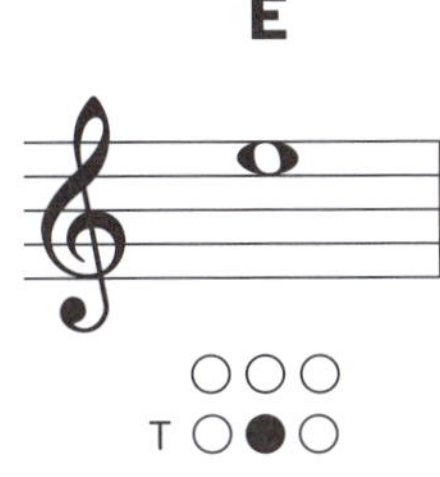

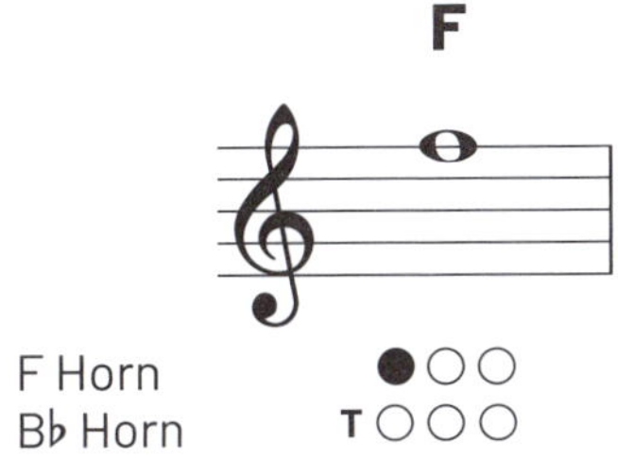

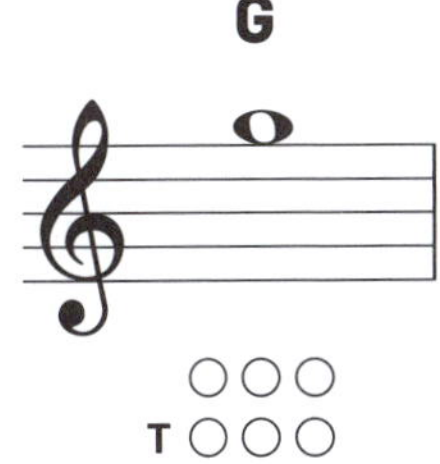

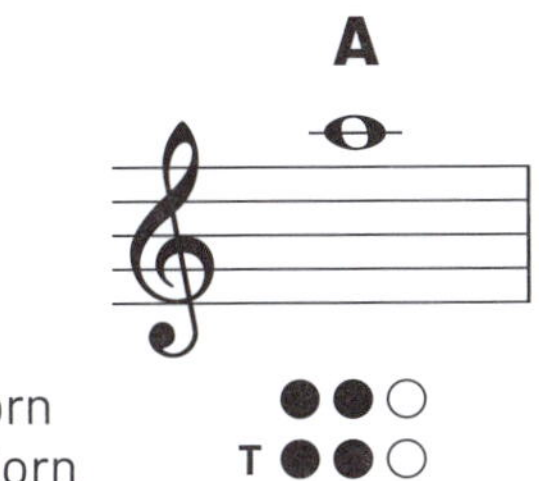

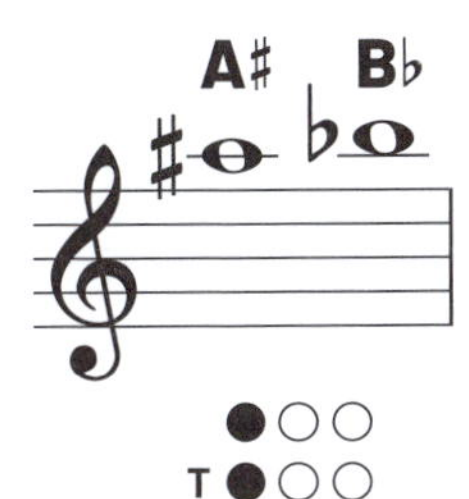

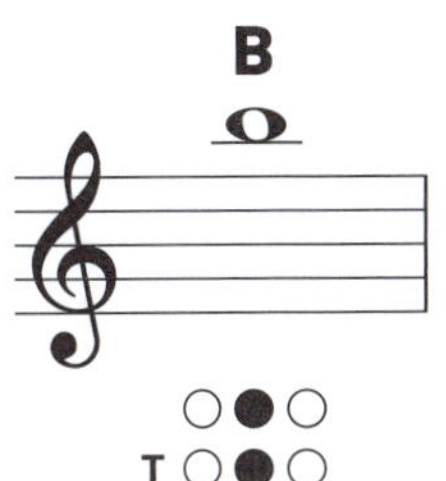

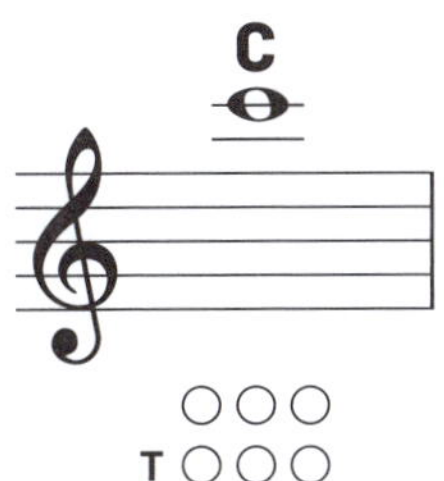

Reference Index

Definitions (pg.)

Book 1 Review

Composers

World Music